MW01205036

2 00

FORENSIC SCIENCE INVESTIGATED

CRIME|LABS

WRITTEN BY:
Rebecca Stefoff

mc Marshall Cavendish
Benchmark
New York

All websites were available and accurate when this book was sent to press.

LIBRARY OF CONGRESS CATALOGING-IN-PUBLICATION DATA
Stefoff, Rebecca
Crime labs / Rebecca Stefoff.
p. cm. — (Forensic science investigated ; 2)
Includes bibliographical references and index.
ISBN 978-0-7614-4140-3
1. Crime laboratories—Juvenile literature. 2. Forensic sciences—Juvenile literature.
I. Title.
HV8073.8.S738 2011
363.25—dc22
2010010536

EDITOR: Christina Gardeski   PUBLISHER: Michelle Bisson
ART DIRECTOR: Anahid Hamparian   SERIES DESIGNER: Kristen Branch

Photo Research by Lindsay Aveilhe
Cover photo by Mario Villafuerte/Getty Images
The photographs in this book are used with permission and through the courtesy of: iStockPhoto (David Marchal): pp. 1, 3; Photo Researchers: p. 4; Bob Krist/Corbis: p. 7; Getty Images: p. 8; Tucson Citizen, Renee Bracamonte/AP Photo: p. 11; Universal/The Kobal Collection: p. 12; Collection Roger-Viollet/The Image Works: p. 15; Courtesy of The Bancroft Library, UC Berkeley: p. 18; Photo by NY Daily News Archive via Getty Images: p. 23; Courtesy FBI: p. 25; Photo Researchers: p. 26; Toby Talbot/AP Photo: p. 28; Bruce Halmo, Pool/AP Photo: p. 33; Philippe Psaila/Photo Researchers, Inc.: p. 35; Daniel Gluskoter/Pool/epa/Corbis: p. 37; Valerie Macon/ Sipa Press/0612071917: p. 40; Ann Johansson/Corbis: p. 44; Jim Varney/Photo Researchers: p. 49; Valerie Macon/Sipa Press: p. 52; The Charlotte Observer, Diedra Laird/AP Photo: p. 61; Anna Clopet/Corbis: p. 62; Newscom: p. 65; Kirsty Wigglesworth/PA Photos/Landov: p. 68; Mark Peterson/Corbis: p. 72; Tek Image/Photo Researchers, Inc.: p. 74; Newscom: p. 77; Marcio Jose Sanchez/AP Photo: p. 78; Daily Oklahoman, Nate Billings, File/AP Photo: p. 82.

Printed in Malaysia (T)
1 3 5 6 4 2
Cover: A forensic scientist at the Louisiana State Crime Lab collects a DNA sample.

CONTENTS

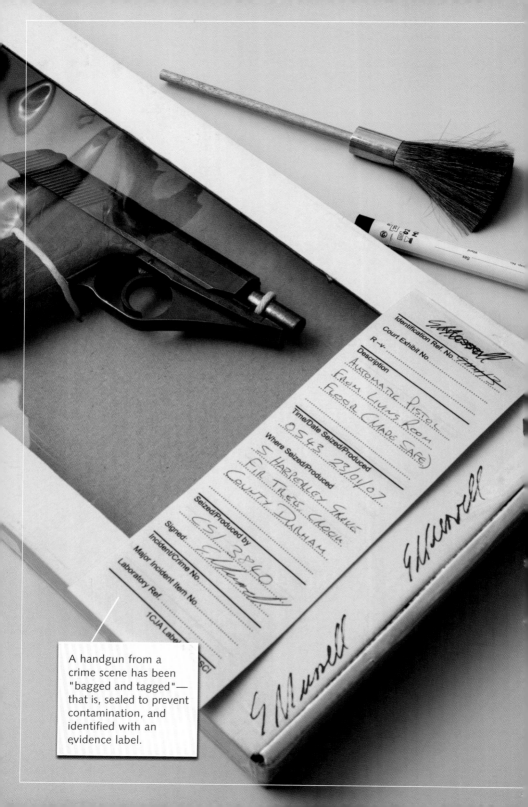

Identification Ref. No. ....

Court Exhibit No ....

R −v− ....

Description
...AUTOMATIC PISTOL...
...FROM LIVING ROOM...
...FLOOR (MADE SAFE)...

Time/Date Seized/Produced
...0543...23/01/07...

Where Seized/Produced
...S. HARDKELEY STREE...
...F.IR. TREET CROOK...
...COUNTY DURHAM...

Seized/Produced by
...CSI 38240...

Signed ....

Incident/Crime No ....

Major Incident Item No ....

Laboratory Ref. ....

TCJA Label ....

A handgun from a
crime scene has been
"bagged and tagged"—
that is, sealed to prevent
contamination, and
identified with an
evidence label.

WHAT IS FORENSICS?

"LET'S GET THIS EVIDENCE TO THE LAB!"

You are likely to hear that line in almost any crime show or movie these days. Whether the evidence is a bullet found at the scene of a shooting, a chip of paint from the jeans of a kid who has been struck by a speeding car, or a disposable coffee cup crumpled and thrown away by a suspect under investigation, police or detectives rush it to a crime lab, where it gives up its secrets. In the hands of white-coated lab technicians, that bullet, paint chip, or crumpled cup points straight to the criminal.

Real-life criminal investigation is almost never as fast and easy as it looks in TV shows and movies. On television, DNA tests are completed almost instantly, but in reality they can take days, weeks, or even months. The men and women who work in crime labs, examining evidence from crime scenes and victims' bodies, do not always come up with the "perfect match" to a fingerprint or a strand of hair. Yet one thing is true in the real world *and* the world of entertainment: many crimes today are solved in the laboratory, thanks to **forensic science**.

Forensic science is the use of scientific methods and tools to investigate crimes and bring suspects to trial. The term "forensic" comes from ancient Rome, where people debated matters of law in a public meeting place called the Forum. The Latin word *forum* gave rise to *forensic*, meaning "relating to courts of law or to public debate."

Today the term **forensics** has several meanings. One is the art of speaking in debates, which is why some schools have forensics clubs or teams for students who want to learn debating skills. The best-known meaning of "forensics," though, is crime solving through forensic science.

Fascination with forensics explains the popularity of many TV shows, movies, and books, but crime and science have been linked for a long time. The first science used in criminal investigation was medicine, and one of the earliest reports of forensic medicine comes from ancient Rome. In 44 BCE, the Roman leader Julius Caesar was stabbed to death not far from the Forum. A physician named Antistius examined the body and found that Caesar had received twenty-three stab wounds, but only one wound was fatal.

▲ In modern Rome, marble columns and worn foundations still stand on the site of the ancient Roman Forum, the source of the word "forensics."

Antistius had performed one of history's first recorded postmortem examinations, in which a physician looks at a body to find out how the person died. But forensics has always had limits. Antistius could point out the chest wound that had killed Caesar, but he could not say who had struck the deadly blow.

Death in its many forms inspired the first forensic manuals. The oldest one was published in China in 1248. Called *Hsi duan Yu* (The Washing Away of Wrongs), it tells how the bodies of people who have been strangled differ from drowning victims. When a corpse is recovered from the water, says the manual, officers of the law should examine the tissues and small bones in the neck. Torn tissues and broken bones show that the victim met with foul play before being thrown into the water.

Poison became another landmark in the history of forensics in 1813, when Mathieu Orfila, a professor of medical and forensic chemistry at the University of Paris, published *Traité des poisons* (A Treatise on Poisons). Orfila described the deadly effects of various mineral, vegetable, and animal substances. He laid the

▲ Science convicted Marie LaFarge of murdering her husband.

foundation of the modern science of **toxicology**, the branch of forensics that deals with poisons, drugs, and their effects on the human body.

As France's most famous expert on poisons, Orfila played a part in an 1840 criminal trial that received wide publicity. A widow named Marie LaFarge was accused of poisoning her husband. Orfila testified that when he examined LaFarge's corpse he found arsenic in the stomach. Marie LaFarge insisted that she had not fed the arsenic to her husband, and that he must have eaten it while away from home. The court, however, sentenced her to life imprisonment. Pardoned in 1850 after ten years in prison, Marie LaFarge died the next year, claiming innocence to the end.

Cases such as the LaFarge trial highlighted the growing use of medical evidence in criminal investigations and trials. Courts were recognizing other kinds of forensic evidence, too. In 1784 a British murder case had been decided by physical evidence. The torn edge of a piece of newspaper found in the pocket of a suspect named John Toms matched the torn edge of a ball of paper found in the wound of a man who had been killed by a pistol shot to the head (at the time people used rolled pieces of cloth or paper, called wadding, to hold bullets firmly in gun barrels). Toms was declared guilty of murder. In 1835, an officer of Scotland Yard, Britain's famous police division, caught a murderer by using a flaw on the fatal bullet to trace the bullet to its maker. Such cases marked the birth of ballistics, the branch of forensics that deals with firearms.

Not all forensic developments involved murder. Science also helped solve crimes such as arson and forgery. By the early nineteenth century, chemists had developed the first tests to identify certain dyes used in ink. Experts could then determine the age and chemical makeup of the ink on documents, such as wills and valuable manuscripts, that were suspected of being fakes. Forensics later expanded to include contributions from other sciences, including odontology, the study of teeth and bite marks; entomology, the study of insects and their life cycles; pathology, the study of disease and injury, which focuses on finding how someone died; and physical anthropology, the study of similarities and differences among human bodies, which can help investigators identify bodies of unknown crime victims.

Forensics started to become a regular part of police work at the end of the nineteenth century, after an Austrian law professor named Hans Gross published a two-volume handbook on the subject in 1893. Gross's book, usually referred to as *Criminal Investigation*, brought together all the many techniques that scientists and law enforcers had developed for examining the physical evidence of crime—bloodstains, bullets, and more. Police departments started using *Criminal Investigation* to train officers. The book entered law school courses as well.

Modern forensics specialists regard Hans Gross as the founder of their profession. Among other contributions, Gross invented the word **criminalistics**. He used it to refer to the general study of crime or criminals. Today, however, criminalistics has a narrower, more specific meaning. It refers to the collection, protection, and examination of physical evidence from crime scenes. After a crime scene has been photographed and measured and recorded in detail, the evidence is removed for scientific study in a forensic laboratory, or crime lab. From simple beginnings more than a century ago, the crime lab has grown into a wonderland of computers and high-tech scientific equipment, run by well-trained criminalists, to meet the needs of the twenty-first century.

▲ A DNA specialist swabs a bullet casing. Skin cells or blood traces on the casing may yield the DNA profile of someone involved in the crime.

Sherlock Holmes, portrayed here by actor Basil Rathbone, used forensics to solve some fictional mysteries.

CHAPTER ONE

THE RISE OF THE FORENSIC LABORATORY

▼ SHERLOCK HOLMES IS PROBABLY THE most famous imaginary detective in the world. Holmes solved many cases through sheer brain power and logical thought. But he also spent a lot of time crawling around on his hands and knees with a magnifying glass, finding evidence such as tobacco ash, bullets, and the prints left by bicycle tires. He then studied that evidence according to the principles of science.

British writer Arthur Conan Doyle introduced Holmes to the world in 1887, in a tale called *A Study in Scarlet*. The great detective first appears in "the chemical laboratory up at the hospital." He has just invented a new chemical test to show whether a stain on a suspect's clothing is blood or something else, such as rust or mud. "Criminal cases," declares Holmes, "are continually hinging upon that one point." Dr. Watson, who shares an apartment with Holmes in London, discovers that the detective also likes to do chemical experiments at home. At times he turns their residence into something like a forensic laboratory.

When Doyle created Sherlock Holmes, the use of science in criminal investigation was still a fairly new idea—and one that fascinated readers, as it continues to do today. The term "forensics" had not come into use in Doyle's time, but Sherlock Holmes was a forensic scientist. When Holmes carefully examined physical evidence such as footprints and bullets, or performed a chemical experiment to answer a question about a crime, he was using the best criminalistic practices known in the late nineteenth century. Today's newest state-of-the-art forensic labs seem very different from Holmes's magnifying glass and chemistry set, but they serve the same purpose. They focus the eye of science on the evidence of crimes.

▶ EARLY FORENSIC LABORATORIES

Science and law meet in the crime or forensics laboratory. Whether the crime lab is as small as a tabletop or as big as a city block, it is a place set aside for the scientific study of items connected with crimes, legal cases, or the justice system.

The first crime labs were established in the early twentieth century. As knowledge of criminalistics and forensics advanced over the years, labs grew larger and more complex.

LOCARD'S LABORATORY

The world's first forensic laboratory was the creation of Edmond Locard of France, one of the pioneers of forensic science. His career was the perfect example of how forensics unites science—in this case, medical science—with the law.

Locard was born in the French city of Lyon in 1877. He was sixteen when Hans Gross published *Criminal Investigation*, the book that launched the organized study and practice of forensics. Locard received a medical degree in 1902. Especially interested in medicine as it applied to legal questions, he had written a student

▲ French physician and lawyer Edmond Locard proved the value of the crime lab.

research paper on that topic. A few years after Locard became a medical doctor, he took up the study of law. By 1907 he was qualified to practice both law and medicine.

After completing his legal education, Locard continued to study on his own, traveling to many European cities to learn from researchers in criminalistics and to see the different ways in which police departments were starting to use forensic science. He also traveled to the United States to observe how the large urban police departments of Chicago and New York dealt with evidence from crime scenes.

When Locard returned to Lyon in 1910, he was full of enthusiasm for the new science of forensics. The Lyon police department did not have a forensic department or laboratory, so Locard persuaded local officials to let him start one. Locard set up a small laboratory in a few rooms in the attic above the courthouse. There he had microscopes to examine evidence, as well as equipment and supplies to perform chemical tests.

Two years later, after a local woman was found strangled to death, Locard achieved a major triumph. He told police to scrape beneath the fingernails of the dead woman's lover, and there they found tiny bits of face powder and skin. Using microscopic studies, Locard demonstrated that those particles matched the victim's powder and skin. His forensic examination of the evidence found under the man's nails helped convict the man of murder.

That same year officials in Lyon formally recognized Locard's operation as the police department's crime laboratory—the first such laboratory in the world. In the years that followed, criminalists and police officers from many countries came to study with Locard, at Lyon and also at a school of criminalistics that he helped to establish in Switzerland. Locard led a movement to train police in scientific techniques, and his Lyon laboratory became the model for crime labs in police departments around the world.

One of Locard's most important contributions to forensic science is known as "Locard's exchange principle." When teaching or writing about criminalistics, Locard stressed the idea that criminals leave traces of themselves at crime scenes, and crime scenes or victims leave traces on the criminals. In other words, evidence is exchanged.

The evidence that is exchanged does not have to be as noticeable and clear as a set of bloody fingerprints. It may be a single hair that fell from a killer's head onto his victim's lifeless body, or a few grains of plant pollen that stuck to a killer's shoes as he walked away from the field in which he'd dumped a corpse. The key is that some kind of physical clue—known as trace evidence—links a criminal to the scenes of his or her crimes. The job of the criminalist is to find and analyze that evidence.

THE BEGINNINGS OF FORENSICS IN THE UNITED STATES

Another important early crime lab was created in Berkeley, California, by a law enforcement officer named August Vollmer. In 1905 Vollmer was elected town marshal of the community. Four years later Berkeley established a police department, and Vollmer became the city's first chief of police. He

▲ August Vollmer founded America's first crime labs. Around the time he was photographed in 1925, he was creating a laboratory for the Berkeley, California, police department.

remained in charge of the Berkeley police force until 1932, except for 1923–1924, when he ran the police department in Los Angeles.

Vollmer had read Hans Gross's *Criminal Investigation* and other early works by European criminalists. He wanted to modernize police work in the United States by introducing the European methods of scientifically studying crime scene evidence. In Los Angeles in 1923, Vollmer established America's first forensic laboratory. After returning to Berkeley, he set up a forensics laboratory there, too. The Berkeley lab became a leading center of forensics in the United States.

As early as 1916 Vollmer had begun teaching summer classes in forensic science for police officers at the University of California in Berkeley. Eventually these classes grew into a complete degree program, and in 1950 the university founded its School of Criminology. Paul Kirk, a forensic specialist whom Vollmer had trained, taught criminalistics there. Vollmer and Kirk educated several generations of criminalists in such subjects as fingerprint analysis and ballistics. They also introduced new methods of filing information about crimes, so that investigators could easily find and compare similar cases.

Two years after Vollmer created America's first police department crime laboratory, the country's first private forensics lab opened in New York City.

Called the Bureau of Forensic Ballistics, it was a business operated by a military historian and former army officer named Calvin Goddard, together with several colleagues. The Bureau of Forensic Ballistics provided services to individuals and police departments all over the country. The chief work of the bureau, as its name suggests, was in ballistics.

Ballistics focuses on the marks that are left on bullets as they pass through a firearm when it is fired. The idea behind forensic ballistics is that the insides of gun barrels have slight irregularities in their surfaces. Because of this, each firearm leaves a distinctive and unique pattern of marks on the bullets that pass through it. These marks, which are called striations or striae, can be used to tell whether two bullets were fired from the same gun or from different guns.

Goddard was an expert in examining striations. Together with a chemist named Philip Gravelle, Goddard developed a tool called the comparison microscope, which let him view two objects at once through magnifying lenses. He could place a bullet from a crime scene or a victim next to a bullet test-fired from a gun found by police in a suspect's pocket, then examine the pair of bullets in detail side by side. If the same pattern appeared on both bullets, Goddard could declare that the fatal bullet had come from the suspect's gun.

In 1930 Goddard was made the director of a new ballistics laboratory that was connected with the School of Law at Northwestern University near Chicago. This lab expanded beyond ballistics to provide a range of forensic services, such as analyzing fingerprints, bloodstains, and tire tracks. Goddard went on to help the Federal Bureau of Investigation (FBI) set up its first crime lab. He then returned to practicing forensic ballistics in New York, and later he taught that subject to criminalists in the U.S. military.

▶ THE FBI AND FORENSICS

At the same time that forensic science was developing in the United States, a national law enforcement agency was taking shape. This process started in the late nineteenth century, when the federal, or national, government gained the authority to investigate interstate crimes—that is, crimes that cross state lines.

At first, interstate law enforcement was the responsibility of the Secret Service, which was part of the U.S. Treasury Department. In 1908 President Theodore Roosevelt shifted the responsibility for interstate law enforcement to a new agency called the Bureau of Investigation, which was part of the Justice Department. From a staff of twelve investigators, called special agents, the bureau grew to more than three hundred special agents before 1920.

ONE BIG, BLOODY CASE in the career of ballistics expert Calvin Goddard took place in Chicago on February 14, 1929. The event, quickly named the St. Valentine's Day massacre, helped fuel the growth of the national law enforcement agency that is now known as the Federal Bureau of Investigation.

The massacre was part of a battle for control of the profitable trade in illegal liquor. A constitutional amendment in effect between 1929 and 1933 outlawed the sale of alcoholic drinks in the United States. Alcoholic drinks were manufactured in secret factories or smuggled into the country from Canada or Europe. Criminal gangs controlled the trade in these illegal beverages.

Al Capone and George "Bugs" Moran ran rival gangs in Chicago. By early 1929 Moran's gang had hijacked Capone's liquor shipments and killed some of his men. On the day of the massacre, seven Moran men were in a warehouse where the gang stored liquor. Suddenly four men—some of them wearing police uniforms—burst in and shot the Moran men to death.

The Chicago police insisted that they had played no part in the incident. The shooters must have been rival gangsters disguised in police uniforms. The obvious suspect was Al Capone, but he was in Miami at the time of the shootings.

Ballistics expert Calvin Goddard examined bullets and shell casings from the crime scene and found that they had been fired from Thompson submachine guns, fast-firing weapons used by both gangsters and the Chicago police.

THE ST. VALENTINE'S DAY MASSACRE, AS RE-ENACTED BY THE CHICAGO AUTHORITIES WHO INVESTIGATED THE CASE.

Goddard got hold of all the Thompson guns used by police, test-fired those guns, and then compared the bullets from the massacre with all the bullets he had fired from the guns of the Chicago Police Department. He found no matches. The police force was cleared of suspicion.

But who *was* responsible for the St. Valentine's Day massacre?

Two of Capone's henchmen were charged, but one was murdered before the trial. The other was saved when his girlfriend gave him an alibi. Another suspect, Fred "Killer" Burke, dropped out of sight. In late 1929 police located Burke in Michigan. Goddard proved that two sub-machine guns found in Burke's hideout had been used in the February killings. Burke, however, was tried, convicted, and imprisoned for a crime he committed months after the massacre—the murder of a Michigan policeman.

Over the years, researchers have debated the St. Valentine's Day massacre. Most think that Al Capone ordered the killings, but the shooters' identities have never been proven. The massacre did, however, put ballistics into the newspaper headlines. Goddard's work on the case led Chicago's law enforcement and community leaders to establish a major new forensics lab, directed by Goddard, at Northwestern University.

A new era began for the bureau when J. Edgar Hoover became its director in 1924. Hoover would remain in charge of the FBI for forty-eight years. Some of his most important steps, though, took place in the early years. Hoover fired special agents who held their jobs only because they were related to politicians or people in power, then focused on hiring college-educated special agents. He also introduced forensic science to the bureau. In 1932, with advice from ballistics expert Calvin Goddard, Hoover established a forensic lab called the Technical Laboratory in Washington, D.C. This facility was intended to help bureau agents investigate and solve crimes.

The new lab was neither large nor impressive. It was a single room, chosen to be the lab because it had a sink. The lab's single full-time employee, Charles Appel, had been trained by Goddard. He was equipped with a microscope, a camera, and a few other scientific tools.

In 1935, when Hoover's agency was renamed the Federal Bureau of Investigation, the crime lab was important to the director as a publicity tool. It let Hoover boast that the FBI was using advanced crime-solving equipment and techniques, even though there were better police labs elsewhere. In the years that followed, however, the FBI lab gained size, staff, and importance, until it became a world leader in forensic procedures and techniques.

▲ The FBI, the national law enforcement agency of the United States, gained its first crime lab—a single room with a sink and a few pieces of equipment—in 1932.

When the FBI's crime lab was new, in the 1930s, it handled about two hundred pieces of evidence a year. Today the FBI lab receives an average of six hundred pieces of new evidence every day from all over the United States and the world. Forensics has grown into a major part of modern law enforcement, and the FBI lab has grown along with it.

Fingerprints are distinctive patterns left by skin oils. Dusting with powder brings latent, or invisible, prints to light.

CHAPTER TWO

CRIME LABS AND EVIDENCE

▼ FORENSIC LABORATORIES ARE EITHER

public labs or private. Each type is funded from a different source. Public and private labs may operate somewhat differently, as well, even though they use the same equipment and techniques. All crime labs, however, follow the same basic principles for handling physical evidence in a criminal investigation.

▶ PUBLIC LABS

Public labs are paid for with public funds. They are government agencies, whether local, state, or federal, and are a form of civil service. City police departments, county sheriff's departments, state police departments, and regional law enforcement organizations are among the agencies that may operate public or civil service crime labs.

A civil service crime lab may be part of the office of the **medical examiner (ME)**. An ME is a public official who is also a doctor and who works within the justice system. The ME's job is to perform an **autopsy** on the body of anyone who has died in mysterious circumstances or for unknown reasons, to find out how the person died. If the death is found to be homicide, the autopsy may also provide evidence that will help investigators find the killer.

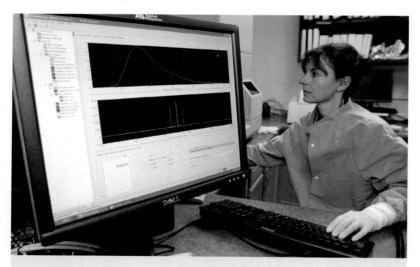

▲ A large computer screen shows the progress of a DNA analysis. The DNA profile being developed will be useful only if investigators can match it to a suspect.

When bodies are turned over to an ME for autopsy, they are kept in a special type of laboratory called a **morgue**, which has refrigerated storage lockers and surgical equipment designed for dissecting bodies, or cutting them open. In many police and sheriff's departments, the forensic evidence lab is located in the same building as the morgue, or nearby.

Federal government agencies operate civil service crime labs, too. The FBI was the first federal agency to open a forensic laboratory. Today the U.S. Postal Service, the Drug Enforcement Agency, and the Bureau of Alcohol, Tobacco, Firearms, and Explosives all have crime labs of their own, where specialists at each of these agencies can study evidence.

▶ PRIVATE LABS

Private forensic laboratories are businesses that provide services to customers for a fee. Those customers include companies and individuals. Government or public agencies such as police departments also make use of private, commercial labs. In some cases, there may be no public lab available to do the necessary work, or the public lab may have a backlog of assignments. A police or sheriff's department may also turn to a private lab for a forensic test or examination that is extremely complex and unusual, if the available public labs lack the necessary equipment or skill.

Private labs are not necessarily full-time forensic labs. Often they do work that is not related to criminal cases or investigations. In a private or commercial lab, technicians may perform the same scientific tests that are used in criminal cases, but for other reasons. One such reason is employment testing. Many employers require people who apply for jobs to take drug tests, which usually involve a sample of urine. The samples are sent for testing to private laboratories. The results of the tests show whether the job seeker used illegal drugs such as heroin and marijuana, or legal ones such as alcohol, within certain time periods before giving the sample. Athletes are frequently tested, too, to check whether they have used banned performance-enhancing substances such as steroids.

DNA testing is another scientific procedure that may be performed either for forensic reasons or for other purposes. Forensic uses of DNA include identifying an unrecognizable body, showing that a suspect left traces of himself or herself (saliva, blood, or hair) on a weapon or at a crime scene, and linking a killer or rapist to a victim through skin cells or body fluids left on the victim.

People have their DNA tested for nonforensic reasons, too. They ask a lab to test a sample of their DNA (usually collected from the inside of the cheek, with a simple swipe of a cotton-tipped swab) to learn whether their genetic heritage includes genes that put them at higher risk for certain diseases. DNA testing can also prove that a child is—or is not—the son or daughter of a specific person. Finally, some labs offer "ethnic origins" or "ethnic ancestry" tests that compare customers' DNA samples to large databases of genetic information from around the world. These tests tell the customers what population groups, such as western Mediterranean people or central Asian people, make up their genetic heritage.

▶ HOW CRIME LABS HANDLE EVIDENCE

Whether a crime lab is public or private, large or small, it follows some universal principles about how evidence should be handled, and how it can be used. One of the most important of these principles is known as the **chain of custody**.

CHAIN OF CUSTODY

The chain of custody is made up of people—the individuals who have custody, or control, of each piece of physical evidence, starting from the moment it is discovered. A good chain of custody makes it clear who was responsible for the evidence, and where the item was located, at each moment of time right up to the trial and beyond.

The chain of custody is not simply a list of names, however. It also specifies where and how the evidence

EVIDENCE IN CRIMINAL investigations or trials is sometimes sent to private labs for testing. In such cases, the lab may be working for either of the two sides in a trial, the defense or the prosecution.

The defense is the side that represents the defendant, the person who is on trial. The defense's mission is to persuade a judge or jury that the defendant is innocent. The prosecution, headed by a public official called a prosecutor, represents the state, or the law. The prosecution charges the defendant with the offense. When the case goes to trial, the prosecution's mission is to demonstrate that the defendant is guilty.

Police and prosecutors usually rely on public or government forensic labs to analyze crime evidence. Sometimes, however, the prosecution may turn to private laboratories—for example, the prosecution may want a private lab to retest the public lab's results. If both a police department lab and a private lab agree, for example, that a bullet removed from the heart of a homicide victim came from a suspect's gun, the case against that suspect is stronger than it would have been if just one lab had been used. On the other hand, the prosecution has no way of knowing whether the results found by a second, private lab will agree with the those of the public lab. Often prosecutors decide to stick with one set of experts.

Defendants have the right to seek expert interpretation of the evidence in their cases. A defendant's lawyers may ask to have the evidence retested at an independent

MARC LeBEAU, CHIEF CHEMIST AT THE FBI LAB, ANSWERS QUESTIONS ABOUT A VIAL OF BLOOD DURING A *2007* MURDER TRIAL.

laboratory. This is so common that most of the forensic work done by private labs in criminal cases is performed for defendants, not prosecutors.

A second test or examination of the evidence may confirm the results of the first examination. Sometimes, however, the results are different—or the experts can interpret the results in different ways. Many questions in forensic science cannot be answered with a simple yes or no. The answers are in shades of gray rather than in black and white.

When talking about trace evidence, for example, experts rarely use the word "match" with respect to two hairs that look as if they came from the same person, or to describe the result of a comparison between a carpet fiber found on a victim's clothing and the carpet in a suspect's house. Experienced forensic examiners will probably use more precise words, such as "the materials could have come from the same source" or "there is a high likelihood of the same origin." For this reason, when a trial includes forensic evidence, the expert witnesses who testify for the defense may disagree with those who testify for the prosecution. Even though both sides examined the same evidence, the experts interpreted it differently.

was stored while each individual had custody of it, as well as what tests were performed on the evidence at each stage of the chain and any damage that occurred to it. If something goes wrong with a piece of evidence—if, for example, the evidence disappears, or is damaged—the chain of custody tells the authorities who slipped up.

The purpose of the chain of custody is to prevent evidence from being lost, stolen, or damaged. But beyond simply protecting the evidence, the chain of custody is vitally important when a case comes to trial. An unbroken chain makes it much harder for the defense team to persuade a jury that the evidence *might* have been faked, tampered with, or planted on the defendant.

The chain works like this: When a criminalist, detective, or police officer collects a piece of evidence, that evidence is immediately placed in a sealed bag or wrapper. The person who collected the item signs the bag or wrapper, adding the date and time. Then, when the evidence is turned over to another person, the first person signs again, with the time, to show that he or she is giving up custody of the evidence. The person who is taking custody also signs and includes the time.

The same thing happens whenever any piece of evidence is moved or changes hands. If police find a face mask lying on the floor of a bank that has just

▲ Breaking the seal on an evidence bag, a lab technician prepares to study material from a crime scene. Gloves protect the evidence from the technician's DNA and fingerprints.

been robbed, for example, the chain of custody for the mask might start with the crime scene investigator who first touches the mask:

- The investigator bags the mask and hands it to the driver of the police van that carries evidence from the crime scene.
- The driver turns the item over to the clerk whose job is to check evidence into a secure storage facility at the police lab.
- Later the criminalist who is to examine the mask for fingerprints signs for the item,

which is then removed from evidence storage and taken to the fingerprint lab.

• Next to sign for the item is the DNA technician whose job is to try to recover a sample of the bank robber's DNA from skin cells on the inside of the mask.

• The DNA technician then returns the mask to the clerk at the storage facility, who deposits the item in its secure place.

• Finally, a detective signs for the mask and takes it to court, where it is introduced as evidence.

Even the smallest break in the chain of custody can lead to disaster in court. In the 1995 trial of O.J. Simpson, a former football star who was charged with murdering his wife and one of her friends, the defense attorneys hammered relentlessly on weaknesses in the chain of custody recorded by the Los Angeles Police Department (LAPD).

The biggest problem concerned a sample of Simpson's blood that was taken by police so that it could be compared with blood from the crime scene. The police nurse who drew the sample from Simpson did not measure the amount of blood he took. Later he testified that it was about 8 cubic centimeters (cc). By the time the case came to trial, however, the LAPD could account for only 6.5 cc of Simpson's blood sample. Although the nurse's figure of 8 cc was only an estimate, the difference between the two numbers gave the defense an opening. Simpson's lawyers argued that the unaccounted-for blood, amounting to about one-quarter of a teaspoon,

▲ These evidence bags were displayed during the homicide trial of former football star O.J. Simpson. Jurors had concerns about how the evidence had been handled.

could have been planted by the police on crime scene evidence to make Simpson look guilty.

Was the unaccounted-for blood in fact missing? No one will ever know, because the chain of evidence did not start with a definite measurement. The defense did not prove that some of Simpson's blood sample had gone missing, that it had been planted on the evidence, or that someone had intended to misuse the sample in that way—but proof was not necessary. Simply by showing that there was a weakness in the chain of custody, the defense raised questions and doubts in the minds of the jurors. When the time came for the verdict, the jury found Simpson not guilty of the double murder.

Crime labs have long used written records with signatures to document the chain of custody. Many labs now also use high-tech equipment and computerized tracking systems. Labels with bar codes can be placed on evidence bags, then scanned whenever the evidence is moved. Radio-frequency identification (RFID) tags, tiny labels that give off radio signals over short distances, can be used to track the movement and location of items of evidence. Such devices, combined with digital ID cards for police and crime lab employees, can create an unbroken electronic chain of custody, showing where a piece of evidence was at any moment, and whose ID was used when a change in custody occurred.

KNOWN AND UNKNOWN

Forensic examiners are always aware that their work may not help solve a crime or mystery. A criminalist can analyze a piece of evidence, but more than analysis may be needed to make that evidence and that analysis useful. The value of a piece of evidence sometimes depends on what it can be compared to.

Take a fingerprint, for example. A crime scene investigator may lift a perfect fingerprint from the handle of a knife that was found in a murdered man's back. That fingerprint becomes evidence. At the time it is collected, it is an unknown—no one can tell just by looking at the fingerprint whose hand it came from. For the print to be meaningful, it must be taken to the lab and compared with fingerprints from people whose identity is known. In forensics, the unknown half of a comparison is the evidence, and the known half is called the **exemplar**.

In the case of the fingerprint on the knife, investigators can look for exemplars in several places. Their first step might be to check the evidence print against a national computerized database of fingerprints. In the United States the Integrated Automated Fingerprint Identification System (IAFIS), operated by the Federal Bureau of Investigation, has been in use since 1999. It is the largest such database in the world, with prints from 55 million people. Prints enter the system when a person is arrested or when someone applies for a job or a license that requires a background check.

IAFIS is more than a digital record of fingerprints. It includes software that can compare an image of an unknown print with the prints in the system. If IAFIS finds a print on record that has the same features as the unknown print, the two are rated as possible or likely matches, depending upon how many features they share. In the case of the man stabbed in the back,

▲ A forensic specialist reviews fingerprints in a national database. After a software program compares unknown prints with the database, an experienced examiner reviews any matches.

investigators will probably check IAFIS to see if there is a match between the fingerprint found on the knife and a print in the system.

If IAFIS has no match for the print, investigators will collect and examine fingerprint samples from the dead man's family, from his known associates, and from anyone who becomes a suspect in the case. If one of those exemplars matches the evidence print on the knife, the investigators have a good lead. They may not know for certain that the person who gave the exemplar print stabbed the man, but they do know that that person handled the knife, and they will demand an explanation.

What if no match for the evidence print is found? In that case, the fingerprint from the knife cannot help identify the man's killer. The print will remain on file, however, in case a matching exemplar turns up later.

For every piece of forensic evidence, there is an exemplar somewhere that investigators hope to find. The exemplar may be specific, such as a fingerprint that points to one individual. Or it may be more general, such as a red paint chip that can be identified as coming from a Ford automobile manufactured in 2002 or 2003. While that identification is not specific, it helps narrow the search. And if police find a suspect who happens to drive such a car, the paint chip adds to the evidence against that suspect.

OUT OR IN?

Even evidence that does not lead investigators to a criminal may be helpful in another way. Think again about that fingerprint found on the knife in the back of a murdered man. Even if investigators are unable to identify the killer through the print, the print can help them rule *out* suspects.

If the fingerprint samples from the dead man's wife, children, and business partner failed to match the fingerprint from the knife, for example, those people would be excluded, or ruled out, as likely killers. When forensic examination removes an exemplar from the pool of possible suspects, an exclusion has taken place.

The opposite of exclusion is inclusion, or the ruling *in* of something. When there is a link between the evidence and an exemplar, inclusion has been shown. Suppose, for example, that two months after the man was found stabbed in the back, a burglar is arrested on the other side of town. When the burglar is fingerprinted, police discover that his fingerprints are not in the IAFIS system, which means that he has not been arrested before. But the prints *do* match the print from the murder knife. The link is inclusionary, and suddenly the arrested man is facing a criminal charge far more serious than burglary.

Crime labs examine a vast variety of evidence. Much of it consists of fingerprints, firearms, small pieces of physical material such as paint chips, and biological evidence such as DNA samples. Anything can become evidence if it is connected with a crime, but even the most advanced tools and techniques in forensic science cannot always answer questions about the evidence. For example, crime lab technicians who perform a dozen tests on a piece of synthetic fiber found on a victim's body may still be unable to say for certain what the fiber is made of or where it came from. In the end, much of the information that comes from crime labs blends human interpretation with scientific analysis.

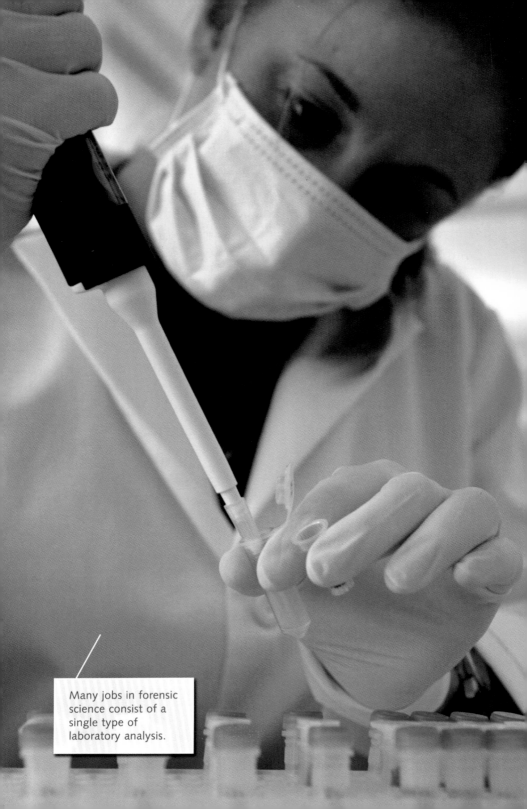

Many jobs in forensic science consist of a single type of laboratory analysis.

CHAPTER THREE

INSIDE THE CRIME LAB

▼ **CRIMINALISTS TODAY ANSWER THE** same questions that have been around since the dawn of forensics. Was this man poisoned? Did this gun fire this bullet? Is the signature on this will genuine or forged? At the same time, crime labs face a steady stream of new challenges. International terrorism, DNA analysis, and computers are just a few of the things that have changed the face of forensics in recent decades. Modern crime labs now use equipment and techniques that no one dreamed of during the early years of forensic science.

▶ **FICTION AND REALITY**

When you hear the words "crime lab," do you picture a sleek setting from a television drama, complete with shiny glass-and-metal workrooms, exotic equipment, and dramatic lighting? Some new crime labs actually look a little like that (but with better lighting). Many are smaller, older, and more crowded.

Some crime lab employees are generalists—that is, "all-purpose" forensic analysts or technicians who work in a number of different sections of the lab or analyze evidence of a variety of types. Most people who work in forensic laboratories, however, are specialists. They are trained and experienced in a particular type of forensic test or analysis, and they perform only that type of work. In contrast to the dramatic variety of tasks performed by crime lab staff on television, the day-to-day work of analysis in a real lab can be, in the words of Dale Nute, a teacher of criminology at Florida State University, "quite repetitive and routine." In addition, crime lab staff are typically responsible for documenting their work, which means spending a fair amount of time at a desk, entering data into a computer.

Crime labs in the real world differ from fictional ones in another important way as well. In shows such as *CSI*, forensic technicians and experts often seem to participate in all phases of an investigation. They collect evidence in the field, examine it in the lab, follow up leads, and interview suspects. In reality, however, investigation and evidence analysis are—or should be—completely separate. Criminalists and crime lab staff do not take part in investigations. Their role is not to solve crimes. It is to collect, preserve, and analyze the evidence without regard for the outcome of the case.

▶ SECTIONS OF A FORENSIC LAB

Large labs usually have separate areas or departments for different kinds of forensic analysis. Smaller labs may have a single work area that is used for a variety of testing procedures, or the labs may perform only a few basic tests and send other work to larger facilities. Some specialized forensic laboratories do just one type of testing: toxicology, for example, or DNA analysis. But a full-service crime lab typically has sections for fingerprints, impressions, firearms, trace evidence, documents, toxicology, blood analysis, and DNA testing. Each of these sections has its own set of equipment and skills.

FINGERPRINTS

A fingerprint is the mark left on a surface by skin oil that collects in the tiny "valleys" between ridges of skin on the fingertips. According to criminalists, the pattern of these ridges and valleys is unique for each person, which is why fingerprints can be used for identification.

The fingerprint section of a crime lab does two things: it develops prints—that is, makes them visible—and identifies them. To develop prints, a forensic examiner may use physical methods, such as brushing the print area with a fine powder that sticks to the oil; chemical methods, such as exposing the prints to gases that will react with the oil; or visual methods, such as using ultraviolet photography to highlight the prints. Not all prints are developed in the crime lab, though. If a print is on something that cannot be moved to the lab, such as a wall, criminalists will develop it at the scene, using the same methods that fingerprint technicians use in the lab.

Once the prints have been developed, whether in the lab or at a crime scene, they must be carefully recorded with detailed photographs. Forensic examiners can scan digital images of prints into computers and use special software to enlarge the prints, remove blurring, and make details clearer.

At this point the print is ready to be identified by means of comparison with known prints. The work may be performed by a software program, but any matches will then be verified by a person trained in fingerprint identification. The strongest identifications use both software and human interpretation.

IMPRESSIONS

Crime scenes often contain impressions, or marks— most commonly footprints and tire marks—left by human activity. Crime scene investigators or technicians measure and photograph impressions, then "lift"

▲ Two methods of capturing a suspect's footprint. On the left, a charge of static electricity has caused dust from the footprint to stick to dark foil. The print on the right has been recorded in a cast.

each impression by making a physical copy of it. Three-dimensional impressions, such as boot prints in gravel or bicycle tire tracks through loose dirt, can be lifted with a plasterlike material called dental stone, which fills an impression without damaging the marks, then hardens into a permanent mold.

Once the photos and impressions have reached the laboratory, forensic examiners study them for information that will help reconstruct the crime scene and identify the participants. "Crime scene reconstruction" means figuring out what happened. Through crime scene reconstruction, investigators hope to determine how many people were present and how they arrived at or left the crime scene. To identify the maker of a given impression, technicians compare the impression of interest to a database of known impressions of, for example, shoe soles or tire tracks. If a shoe or a tire is new, examiners may be able to tell only what brand or style it is. But if the shoe or tire has been used for a while, it may have acquired cuts or patterns of wear that make it highly individual. These distinctive patterns can be matched to a suspect's shoes or tires to produce an identification.

FIREARMS

The firearms division of the crime lab is responsible for examining the evidence that remains from ammunition that has been used in crimes. Whether the weapon in question is a handgun, rifle, or shotgun, the ammunition is called a cartridge, or round, and it consists of the same basic parts. The casing is a shell that holds the other parts—primer, gunpowder, and projectile or projectiles. The primer is a small amount of highly explosive material that explodes when struck by the gun's firing pin. The explosion of the primer ignites the gunpowder, releasing gases that push the projectile out of the cartridge, through the barrel of the gun, and in the direction of the target.

Evidence left after a shooting can consist of the cartridge casings, the projectiles (bullets or shotgun pellets), or both. The goal of investigators is to find out what kind of gun fired the ammunition and, if possible, to link the ammunition to a particular gun. Casings left at a crime scene are useful because they indicate the caliber of the weapon, which corresponds to the size, or diameter, of the ammunition it fires. Bullets also indicate the caliber and type of weapon used. They may also, under the right circumstances, be identified as having been fired from a particular gun.

Firearms examiners use microscopes of several kinds to examine bullets. One kind gives a detailed view that may reveal trace evidence, such as blood or hair, that is invisible to the eye. The comparison microscope, on the other hand, lets the examiner look at two bullets or shell casings side by side. This makes it possible to inspect the evidence for matches in the striations, or microscopic markings on their surfaces.

The Bureau of Alcohol, Tobacco, Firearms, and Explosives maintains a national database of information about casings and bullets that have been used in crimes. A tool called the Integrated Ballistics Identification System (IBIS) gathers digital photographs and data about casings and bullets as these items are examined

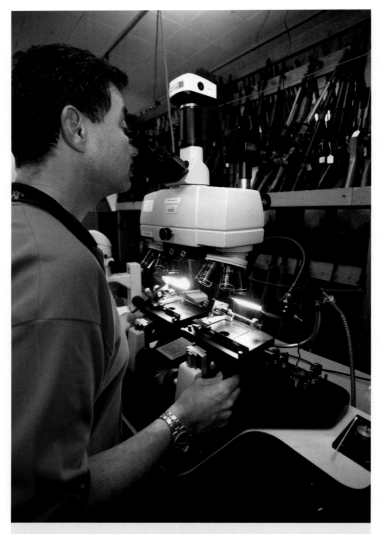

▲ Using a comparison microscope, a ballistics expert examines two bullets to determine whether both were fired by the same gun.

under a computerized microscope, then adds the findings to the database. This allows law enforcement authorities to see the connections among crimes that have been committed with the same weapon, even if the crimes occurred in different parts of the country.

A firearms lab includes a small, secure room for firing weapons into a water tank and at a target. The use of the tank allows the examiner to recover, undamaged, test bullets that have been fired from guns collected during an investigation. The use of the target, at which an "evidence" gun is fired from different distances and at different angles, reveals to the examiner the patterns created by gunpowder or shotgun pellets. Such patterns may indicate how close a shooter was to a victim, for example, or whether the shooter was in front of the victim or to one side.

TRACE EVIDENCE

One of the most varied jobs in forensics is microanalysis. This is the examination of trace evidence, which is a catch-all term for any type of evidence that is small, or microscopic, from a single stray drop of nail polish to a fleck of mud. Items commonly seen in trace evidence exam rooms include hairs, fibers from cloth, dust, soil, bits of paint, and chips of plastic or glass. Some trace evidence is sent to scientific specialists for identification. A botanist, or plant scientist, will probably be asked to identify plant pollen, seeds, or leaves, for example. The eggs or body parts of insects will be sent to an entomologist, a scientist who specializes in insects.

The first step in processing trace evidence is to collect it. While much trace evidence is collected at the crime scene, some of it is harvested in the crime lab. For example, when the clothing worn by a homicide victim reaches the lab, criminalists or analysts will examine it closely under a bright light, sometimes using a magnifying glass. If hairs, carpet fibers, or soil are present on the clothes, these tiny pieces of evidence will be removed for analysis.

There are three primary ways to collect trace evidence. A criminalist or analyst can pick the evidence up with forceps, or tweezers. This approach is ideal for handling small individual pieces of evidence. The second method is called a tape lift. The analyst presses strips of tape against the surface containing the evidence, then pulls them up. Hairs, dust particles, and other bits of trace evidence that have been lifted from the surface stick to the tape. The tape lift is a good way to retrieve trace evidence from surfaces such as glass and upholstery. The third method of collecting trace evidence is to use a vacuum with a clean, new filter that is designed to trap even tiny pieces of material. The vacuum method is a good choice for gathering evidence quickly from a large area. Afterward, however, the analyst may have to sift and sort through a large amount of material, not all of which will be useful as evidence.

MICROANALYSIS

Once the evidence has been collected, microanalysis begins. Forensic examiners use instruments of two general types to study trace evidence. "The workhorse of the trace evidence section is the microscope," says Linda R. Netzel, a crime scene investigator and trace evidence criminalist. A crime lab might contain three or four different kinds of microscopes, each with particular uses.

A stereomicroscope consists of two microscopes arranged side by side. Because the two microscopes focus on the specimen from slightly different angles, the analyst who looks through the eyepiece sees a three-dimensional image. This type of microscope is especially useful for viewing and sorting an array of trace evidence specimens at the same time. To compare two pieces of evidence side by side, the analyst may use a comparison microscope—the same tool used by firearms specialists to compare striations on two bullets.

One of the key tools in trace evidence analysis is the polarized-light microscope, which has a light source to illuminate the specimen, a polarizing filter to highlight extremely tiny features of the specimen, and a rotating platform that lets the analyst turn the specimen and examine it from all angles. Depending on the resources available to the lab, some evidence may be studied with a super-high-powered—and very expensive—electron microscope.

The spectrometer is the trace evidence analyst's other major tool. A spectrometer is any instrument that measures the properties of light, such as wavelength and intensity. Each chemical element or compound produces a distinctive spectrometric reading when light comes from it, passes through it, or is reflected from it. (This is why astronomers can tell what elements make up distant stars, for example.) When an analyst uses a spectrometer to test a sample piece of evidence, he or she learns the sample's chemical fingerprint, or makeup. This can lead to the identification of cosmetics, paints, and other mystery materials.

In addition to knowing how to use scientific equipment, today's trace evidence analysts must know how to use databases. These tools are becoming ever more important. Online databases, as well as reference sources in books and professional journals, contain information about the structure, chemical makeup, and other physical properties of thousands upon thousands of materials, both natural and man-made.

PUTTING EVIDENCE TO THE TEST

To understand how a trace evidence analyst might use laboratory tests and database research, imagine that one piece of evidence found on a murder victim's clothing is a tiny chip of glass. Did the chip come from a window, a drinking glass, a broken picture frame? The type and source of the glass might be valuable clues to the way the victim was killed or the location of the murder.

The analyst will first study the shape of the chip. If it is cube-shaped, the glass was tempered, which means that it was manufactured to break into pieces without sharp edges. Tempered glass is used in automobile windows and glass tabletops. Next the analyst will determine the density of the glass—how heavy it is relative to the space it occupies. Different kinds of glass have different densities. To test the chip, the analyst will place it in a series of liquids of different, known densities. The chip will sink in some of these liquids and float in others. When the chip neither sinks nor floats but simply rests suspended in the middle of the liquid, however, the analyst knows that the chip has the same density as that liquid. The analyst can then look for a match in a reference source that lists the densities of different types of glass.

Another key feature of glass is its refractive index, which tells the analyst the degree to which light bends when passing through the glass. Because different kinds of glass have different refractive indices, this piece of information is an important clue about the source of the mystery chip. Once again, the analyst will place the chip in a series of liquids, each of which has a different, known refractive index. The chip will seem to disappear in a liquid that has a refractive index identical to its own. When the analyst has determined the chip's refractive index, he or she can consult another reference book or database to discover what kinds of glass have the same refractive index as the sample. The answer may tell investigators that the chip on the victim's clothing most likely came from a broken watch, a cooking utensil, a piece of artwork, or something else.

DOCUMENTS

The section of the crime lab devoted to examining documents performs tasks of three general kinds. One is handwriting identification. Investigators might want to know if a signature or other specimen of handwriting is genuine or forged, or if a piece of writing can be matched to a sample of writing from a known suspect. Another task is document recovery. Using combinations of lighting, chemicals, and photography through various filters, document experts may be able to restore the writing on a document that has faded with age or has been erased or burned. Finally, document experts can analyze the documents themselves, to determine what kind of ink, paper, or writing instrument was used to create them.

For decades, typewriters were important in document analysis. Experts learned to tell whether a questioned document had been typed on a particular typewriter, given a sample of material known to have been typed on that machine. Today typewriters have almost disappeared. Most documents that are not handwritten are produced by computer printers or photocopiers. Although it is hard for an examiner to link a document to a particular printer or copier, it may be possible to identify the make and model of the machine that was used to produce the document.

The most important tool for a document examiner is keen eyesight. Even with the help of digital scanners and computer programs, this is one area of forensic science that still relies on the skill and instincts of an experienced examiner. However, document analysts must also know how to use spectrometric equipment to identify the chemical composition of inks and dyes, which in turn can be matched to individual natural substances and commercial products.

TOXICOLOGY

Materials that are believed to be illegal substances, such as drugs, or that may be explosive, toxic, or infectious, are tested in the toxicology section of a crime lab. Like a chemistry or medical lab, a toxicology laboratory must establish strict safety procedures. Toxicological examiners often wear protective gear such as masks and breathing devices.

Forensic toxicologists analyze two general types of evidence: unknown substances and biological specimens. Unknown substances include plant materials (mostly marijuana), powders, and liquids that are either seized from suspects during arrests or found at crime scenes. Biological specimens are samples from crime victims or suspects—urine from a driver suspected to have been drinking heavily, for example, or blood from someone who might have been poisoned or drugged.

A forensic toxicologist's first step is usually a presumptive test, which is a test that will show whether a substance belongs to a general category of drug, poison, or chemical. Once the general category is known, follow-up procedures called confirmatory tests can pin down the exact nature of the substance. Toxicologists can often find the details in chemical makeup that makes one batch of heroin, for example, different from another. This information helps law enforcement link drug crimes or track the activities of drug manufacturers and dealers.

FORENSIC BIOLOGY

Sometimes the evidence in a case includes human tissues (liquids such as blood and other body fluids are considered to be tissues, just like skin and muscle). The examination of tissues is forensic biology. Like toxicology, forensic biology requires examiners to deal with potentially hazardous materials. People who do

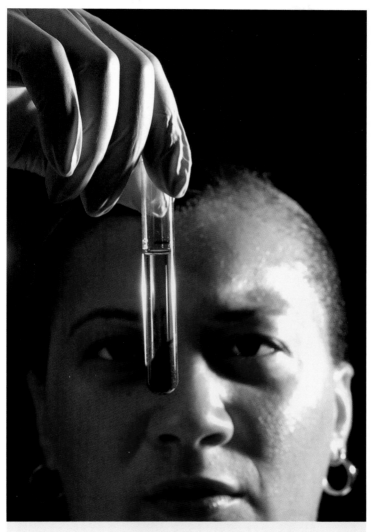

▲ A forensic molecular geneticist in the field of serology—
an expert on DNA and blood—examines a test result.
Her field is one of the busiest in forensic science.

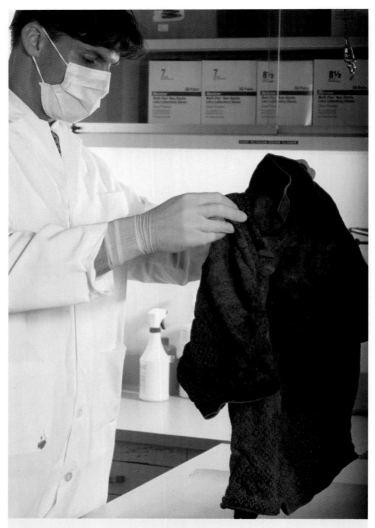

▲ In a lab at the FBI Academy at Quantico, Virginia, a pathologist prepares to take samples of the dried blood crusted on a jacket.

this work follow a number of procedures adopted from medical science.

Serology and DNA analysis are the two main kinds of forensic biology. Serology refers to the study of blood and its properties. A serologist performs tests to tell, for example, whether blood is human or animal, and what its type is. One important role of serology in forensic biology is testing to determine which types of tissue are included in a sample of evidence. Does the sample consist of blood alone, or are skin cells, saliva, or other body fluids present?

Blood tests can be exclusionary, but they cannot be inclusionary. In other words, if a bloodstain on a carpet is Type A blood, but the dead victim lying nearby had Type B blood, the victim is excluded as a possible source of the bloodstains. Someone other than the victim dripped blood on that carpet. But even if the chief suspect in the case has Type B blood, the blood test cannot prove that the bloodstain on the carpet came from the suspect. The stain could have come from anyone with Type B blood. To say with certainty that a given stain is the blood of a particular person, forensic examiners must use DNA testing.

DNA testing creates a profile based on a number of points—usually thirteen—on a person's genetic material, contained in each cell of the body. That profile can then be compared with profiles from other people. Depending

WILDLIFE FORENSICS

PEOPLE ARE NOT the only victims of crime. Poaching, or illegal hunting, kills wildlife and harms the environment. Wildlife crimes are sometimes carried out by people who enjoy the thrill of an illegal hunt, but most such crimes are done for money. They feed a multibillion-dollar international market in exotic pets and in the furs, skins, and body parts of endangered animals. Rhinos in Asia and Africa, for example, have been driven to the brink of distinction by poachers who take their horns because some people superstitiously (and wrongly) believe that powdered rhinoceros horn will have certain effects on their well-being.

A crime lab that is set up to analyze illegal drugs and test human DNA is not equipped to analyze rhino horn, or to tell an endangered bird species from a common one. Since 1989, however, the U.S. Fish and Wildlife Service has operated a forensics laboratory dedicated to wildlife crimes. Located in Ashland, Oregon, it is the world's only wildlife forensics lab. Used by 750 federal agents, the fish and game offices of every state, and 170 foreign countries that want to end the illegal trade in their animals, the National Fish and Wildlife Forensics Laboratory handled a thousand cases in 2009.

The twenty scientists and fifteen nonscientist staff members who work at the Ashland lab have solved many mysteries involving wildlife. Among other things, they have discovered that a sudden flurry of dead animals

By identifying animal parts, forensic experts in Oregon help combat the illegal trade in endangered species.

and birds in Illinois was due to poisoning by a pair of farmers; that three seafood companies were illegally selling the meat of the protected queen conch; and that tribal hunters in Alaska were illegally slaughtering walruses for their tusks. By applying forensic science to wildlife cases, the Ashland lab helps bring to justice those who have committed crimes against the world's animals.

upon how closely two profiles match, analysts calculate how likely it is that they came from the same person.

Many experts say, for example, that the chance of two unrelated people having identical DNA profiles is one in 10 billion. Compared with the total world population of less than 7 billion, 10 billion seems like a very large number. But the experts' statement alone does not prove that it is impossible for two unrelated individuals to have the same DNA profile, just that it is extremely unlikely. If a DNA sample is old, or contains tissue from more than one person, or has been degraded by heat or chemicals, the accuracy of the profile goes down—and the chance of an incorrect match goes up. DNA testing grows ever more powerful, but jurors and the public need to remember that the "DNA matches" seen on television and in the movies are not rock-solid matches. They are statistics.

▶ SAFETY IN THE CRIME LAB

Crime labs are full of dangerous things. Firearms, drugs, poisons, flammable materials, and biological specimens such as blood are just some of the hazardous substances that forensic examiners handle. To work safely with these materials, criminalists follow clear, detailed procedures. They also require special items of safety equipment—in addition to ordinary precautions such as fire extinguishers, which should be present in every workplace.

STAFF SAFETY

Crime labs need some of the same kinds of special safety equipment that are found in hospitals, chemical laboratories, and some manufacturing plants. Emergency showers and eyewash stations, for example, are important. Anyone who is accidentally exposed to a harmful substance should be able to reach one of these stations quickly to rinse the dangerous material out of eyes or off skin and clothing as soon as possible.

Tests involving chemicals or heated minerals may require fume hoods. These are ventilated, cabinet-like workspaces to be used when examiners do anything that may produce dust, chemical vapors, strong smells, or airborne toxins. Powerful built-in fans draw clean air from the room into the cabinet, and the dust particles or vapors are taken up by the room air. The hood then either filters the air to remove the impurities or sends it into ducts to be released outside the room, into a safe place.

Biological safety cabinets are similar to fume hoods. A biological safety cabinet is a protected, well-ventilated workspace for handling hazardous or unknown biological materials. Tissue from the body of a victim, for example, must be handled with a high degree of care because it may be infected with parasites or disease microbes. In some biological safety cabinets, the workspace is not merely ventilated but is

▲ Forensic scientists follow strict safety precautions when handling evidence. Blood samples from a victim, for example, might be infected with disease.

separated from the room by a barrier with sleeves built into it. An examiner can slip his or her hands into the sleeves and handle the specimens inside the cabinet, without any bodily exposure to the air of the cabinet or the dangerous materials being studied.

EVIDENCE SAFETY

Workplace safety in a crime lab applies not only to the people who work there. It applies to the evidence, too. Proper storage space is required so that evidence is protected from contamination. A DNA sample, for example, can be contaminated by hair or skin flakes from a lab worker or by being mixed with another sample. Another example of the danger of evidence contamination would be a small sample of pollen from a murder victim's body. The tiny grains of plant matter, which might hold a vital clue to where the victim was killed, would be useless as evidence if allowed to mix with pollen already present in the air of the lab.

Sealed storage lockers or drawers, some of them refrigerated to hold biological materials, are a necessity in a crime lab. Special storage is also needed for electronic devices and media, such as computer drives and disks, which are an increasingly common type of evidence. Electronics need protection from dust, direct sunlight, extremely hot or cold temperatures, and magnets, which can destroy or garble digital data.

Whatever the evidence, the crime lab must be equipped to preserve it while it is being examined and stored. Evidence that has been damaged or contaminated may be declared useless at trial, no matter how much effort forensic examiners have put into collecting and studying it.

▶ SECURITY IN THE CRIME LAB

Closely related to safety is security, which means protection from threats and harmful acts. Criminals or their associates might try to steal evidence from a crime lab, for example, or tamper with the evidence being held there. Someone who has a grudge against the forensic examiners, or a person who wants to disturb the work of a forensic lab, might plant a bomb or plan some other type of violent attack. The people who work in crime labs, as well as the evidence itself, must be secure from threats like this.

To prevent an armed attack, the designer of a crime lab may specify bulletproof construction materials on the outside of the building, especially in windows and doors. Bulletproof glass or plastic may also be used inside the building, such as between the public entrance and the interior of the lab. Another key security feature is constant video monitoring of entrances and exits. A system of concealed electronic "panic buttons" throughout the building lets laboratory staff call for help if their section of the lab is invaded, perhaps by someone who got into the building by using false identification.

Even landscaping can be a security issue. For example, the U.S. Department of Justice, in its guidelines for designing crime labs, advises against planting shrubs big enough to hide a person and trees that are easy to climb on the grounds close to a lab. The Justice Department also suggests eliminating windowsills that are wide and flat enough to support even a small package, because an attacker could place a bomb on such a ledge. Vents and air conditioners that bring air into the lab should be located in secure, fenced places on the building's outside walls or on its roof, so that no one can attack the lab by putting tear gas or some other substance through an air intake.

▶ THE FBI CRIME LAB

The Federal Bureau of Investigation's crime lab has come a long way from the single room—with a sink— that FBI director J. Edgar Hoover set aside in 1932 for forensic work. The lab has moved to new quarters several times over the years. Since 2003 it has been housed in a specially constructed five-story building in Quantico, Virginia. With 463,000 square feet of laboratories and offices, the lab's total area is bigger than eight American football fields (including the end zones).

The FBI lab consists of many different units, each with its own laboratories. Some of them deal with

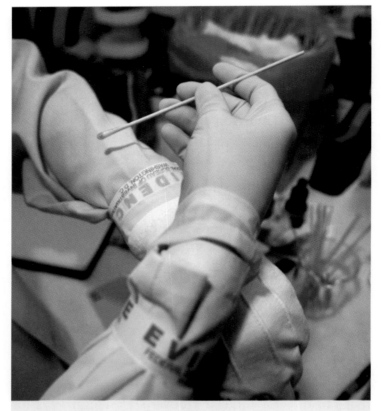

▲ Technicians in DNA labs must take great care to prevent the samples they analyze from becoming contaminated, which can make them useless.

trace evidence, toxicological testing, and fingerprints, just like the typical state police lab or big-city lab. Other parts of the FBI lab, however, are more specialized. The Terrorist Explosive Device Analytical Center (TEDAC), for example, examines the evidence left by terrorist attacks such as bombings of U.S. soldiers by civilians in Iraq. By studying the materials and methods that terrorists used to make the explosives, TEDAC gains information that may help American military and law enforcement teams track down the bomb-makers, or protect themselves more effectively.

Another unit, the Cryptanalysis Team, consists of code breakers who analyze encrypted, or coded, messages. They work on codes used for secret communication by convicts, terrorists, gang members, and gamblers. The Questioned Documents Unit, meanwhile, uses special software to reassemble hundreds of narrow strips of paper, making it possible to read documents that have been run through paper shredders.

About five hundred forensic scientists and special agents work at the FBI lab. In addition to analyzing evidence for federal cases from all over the country, they process evidence from state and local law enforcement agencies in the United States and from other countries. They also provide training courses in forensic procedures. The FBI crime lab is one of the largest and most up-to-date facilities of its kind in the world. However, some serious questions have been raised about the accuracy of its forensic testing.

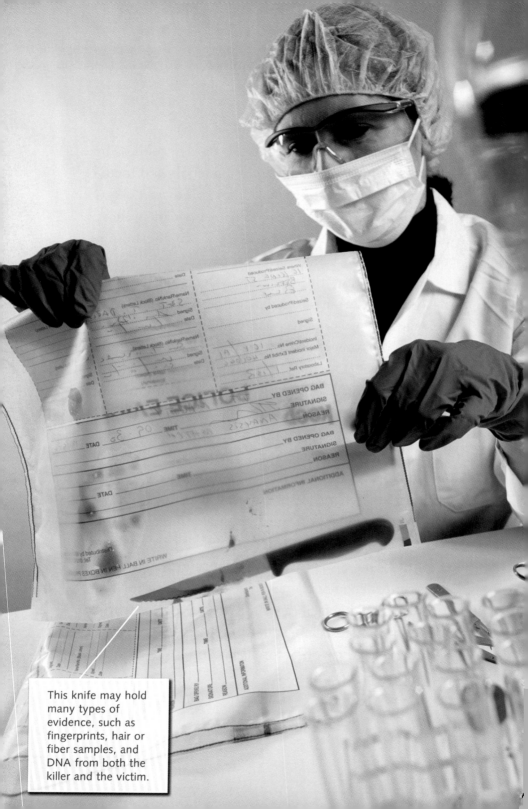

This knife may hold many types of evidence, such as fingerprints, hair or fiber samples, and DNA from both the killer and the victim.

CHAPTER FOUR

CONCERNS AND CHALLENGES

▼ MORE THAN A CENTURY AGO EDMOND

Locard opened the world's first crime lab in France. This event was the beginning of the official relationship between science and crime investigation. Since that time, forensics has been an important part of law enforcement, as well as a subject that fascinates the public.

At the same time, however, experts are debating whether forensic science is as reliable and useful as courts and juries believe it to be. Scandals at the FBI lab and a national report have raised serious questions about the accuracy of the work done in crime labs. Some scientists, lawmakers, and members of the justice system have called for a new look at forensic science in general and at crime laboratories in particular.

▶ PROFESSIONAL STANDARDS

Individual criminalists can be certified by professional organizations, which include the American Board of Criminalistics, the International Association for Identification, and the American College of Forensic Examiners. To qualify for certification, a candidate must complete the required education or training, pass tests, and gain some level of experience in forensic work. Certification is a sign that an individual meets the standards set by his or her professional discipline.

Crime labs can apply for a type of certification, too. It is called accreditation. An accredited laboratory is one that meets certain requirements and follows certain procedures. Those requirements and procedures are set by an organization made up of people who direct crime labs.

The American Society of Crime Laboratory Directors (ASCLD) got its start in 1973, when the Federal Bureau of Investigation invited thirty crime lab directors from around the United States to a conference at the FBI headquarters in Quantico. The goal was to encourage communication and the sharing of knowledge among crime labs at all levels, from local to federal. As a result of the conference, the ASCLD was formed in 1974. Today its members include law enforcement officers, criminalists, chemists, toxicologists, doctors, teachers, and others who are responsible for running

▲ Using a magnifying glass, an analyst checks a bullet for fingerprints. The next step will be a chemical test for prints.

crime labs. The organization has members in many countries outside the United States, including Switzerland, Singapore, China, Costa Rica, and Turkey.

The ASCLD Laboratory Accreditation Board, a separate but related organization, handles the accrediting of crime labs. Any laboratory that wants to be accredited under the program must show that it meets certain requirements and standards. The Laboratory Accreditation Board inspects the lab, interviews its staff and checks the professional standing of each member of the staff, and reviews the lab's procedures for safety, security, and quality control. Accredited labs are reinspected every five years.

An individual criminalist's professional certification is a way of showing any concerned party—such as a judge, juror, defense attorney, or prosecutor—that the criminalist is competent and can be trusted to perform according to professional standards. Accreditation does the same thing for a public or private crime lab.

▶ A NEW ERA IN FORENSICS?

Forensic science has revolutionized law enforcement, but it is not perfect. Even in crime labs with state-of-the-art equipment, people handle evidence and interpret test results—and people make mistakes. But human error may not be the only problem with forensic science today. At the request of the U.S. Congress, a committee

▲ The criminalist who worked here in the San Francisco police lab was accused of stealing cocaine from the evidence she analyzed. Her actions may taint every case in which she was involved.

of experts spent years studying forensic science as it is now practiced in the United States. In 2009 the committee announced that the nation's crime labs were in trouble.

PROBLEMS AND SCANDALS

A biologist named Jacqueline Blake worked in the DNA analysis unit of the Federal Bureau of Investigation from 1988 to 2002. During her last few years with the FBI, she tested evidence from more than a hundred crime scenes.

One evening in 2002, after Blake had left the laboratory, a colleague noticed some test results being displayed on Blake's lab equipment. Blake's work did not appear to follow proper test procedures—it looked as though important steps had been left out. The coworker alerted lab officials, who investigated Blake's work. They discovered that in nearly all her cases, Blake had not carried out the DNA testing properly. Further, she had lied about it, testifying in her lab reports that she had performed the tests correctly.

In 2004 the FBI released a report on Blake's faulty test procedures and her fraudulent claim that she had followed proper procedures. That same year Blake pleaded guilty in court to the misdemeanor charge of providing false statements. She, who resigned from the FBI, was sentenced to two years of probation. Because of this mishandling of evidence, defense attorneys could file appeals, requesting new trials, for people who had been convicted in cases in which Blake's test results were used.

The Blake mess was not the first scandal to taint the FBI crime lab, or the biggest. In the mid–1990s an FBI special agent and chemist named Frederic Whitehurst revealed hundreds of examples of scientific misconduct and forensic fraud that he had observed and documented in the FBI's laboratories. Whitehurst's bombshell greatly embarrassed the FBI, which had called its crime lab one of the best in the world. The U.S. Congress launched an inquiry into the operation of the FBI lab, and as a result the FBI made dozens of major reforms in its procedures, including the firing or reassignment of members of the forensic staff. Among other things, the FBI agreed for the first time to apply for professional accreditation for its labs.

THE PITFALLS OF PROGRESS IN DNA TESTING

The FBI is not the only law enforcement agency that has had problems operating its crime lab. State and local labs have also fumbled the handling of evidence, sometimes through deliberate fraud but often as a result of simple mistakes.

DNA testing has become so important to crime investigation that judges and juries now expect to see DNA evidence in the majority of cases involving serious crimes. Unfortunately, DNA testing is also a very complex process, one that changes often as new equipment and techniques are developed. Few people outside the scientific community understand DNA testing completely, but most think that DNA tests are reliable. People place so much confidence in DNA testing that an improper test can do a lot of damage, as happened in Washington State in 2002.

A forensic scientist at Washington's state police crime lab was testing DNA samples from clothing seized as evidence in two different cases. Because the forsensics specialist failed to sterilize the scissors he had used to cut a piece of cloth out of a sample from one case, before cutting a sample of cloth from the second case, he contaminated at least one of the samples. He then tested a piece of cloth from a garment of a girl whose uncle was accused of having sexually assaulted her. The test revealed DNA, but not from the uncle— it was from a second man.

The second man was completely unconnected to the assault on the girl, but his DNA had been transferred to her clothing by the unsterilized scissors used in the lab work. As a result, there was no usable DNA evidence against the uncle. The uncle had already confessed to the assault, but confession carries less weight in court than physical evidence, because attorneys and jurors know that people sometimes confess to crimes they did not commit, and because defendants sometimes

▲ Frederic Whitehurst, an explosives expert who worked in the FBI crime lab from 1986 to 1998, revealed mistakes and misconduct in the lab's work. He became an activist for forensic reform and stricter standards.

claim that they were pressured to confess. Without DNA from the girl's clothing, the prosecution had no solid physical evidence, so the uncle was convicted on a lesser charge. Instead of twenty-six years in prison, he was sentenced to only sixteen years.

DNA was first used in criminal investigation in the 1980s. Back then, accurate results called for a sample of blood or other body fluid at least the size of a quarter. Science has advanced so much since then that now labs can perform accurate DNA tests on samples of only a few dozen cells, invisible to the naked eye. This level of accuracy makes it possible for labs to get results from samples that would have been much too small only a few years ago.

Unfortunately, a higher level of accuracy also makes it easier for samples to be contaminated by extremely tiny amounts of DNA from other sources. The Seattle crime lab has reported a case in which the lab director was talking with a forensic scientist while the scientist examined evidence. The director's DNA was later found on the evidence, carried there by a microscopic droplet of saliva during the conversation. The more detailed and accurate forensic technology becomes, the more care labs must take to shield evidence from accidental contamination.

▶ REPORT CARD FOR THE NATION'S CRIME LABS
In 2005 the National Academy of Sciences (NAS), an organization made up of scientists from many fields, received an assignment from Congress. Recognizing the ever-growing role of forensics in law enforcement, as well as the potential for mistakes and abuses, Congress asked the NAS, which advises the federal government on scientific matters, to review the overall state of forensic science in the United States.

The NAS appointed a committee of scientists, forensic professionals, and law enforcement personnel.

The committee members spent several years analyzing the scientific literature on forensics, reviewing case histories, inspecting labs, and interviewing people from public and private crime labs, people from all levels of law enforcement, scientists and scholars, crime lab directors, criminalists, and lawyers. In 2009 the committee issued its report under the title *Strengthening Forensic Science in the United States: A Path Forward.*

The report, which is available online, sparked headlines such as "Crime labs are seriously deficient" (NBC), "Science Found Wanting in Nation's Crime Labs" (*The New York Times*), "Crime labs need major overhaul" (CNN), and "Report questions science, reliability of crime lab evidence" (*Los Angeles Times*). As these alarming headlines show, the NAS argued that forensic science is not as certain and reliable as most people believe.

Strengthening Forensic Science pointed to three problem areas:

- The great majority of public crime labs are associated with, or operated by, law enforcement agencies. The close link between crime labs and law enforcement can create a bias, or tilt, in the interpretation of evidence, or put pressure on the forensic examiners to produce results that support the police or the prosecution. The NAS recommended that labs be made independent of law enforcement. Lab directors should be people with a background in science rather than in law enforcement. Forensics should be driven by neutral, scientifically accurate interpretations of evidence, not by the desire to "get convictions."

- Many crime labs are understaffed and overworked, or they operate in crowded facilities, or they lack enough funds to do the best possible job. In addition, labs differ widely in the staff qualifications, equipment quality, and enforcement of procedures. This leads to inconsistencies. It is unfair to defendants that the same evidence could be tested and interpreted quite differently in two different labs. To reform this "badly fragmented" system, the NAS says that all labs, not just some of them, should be accredited, and that a national forensics board should be created to oversee all labs, applying the same standards to each.
- Forensic science is not as well founded as many expert witnesses would like jurors to think. According to the NAS, the most solidly scientific part of forensic science is DNA

testing—when it is properly carried out. Other branches of forensic science, such as fingerprint analysis and ballistics, have been used in laboratories and courts for decades, but they have not undergone strict scientific study by independent scholars. For example, the NAS report pointed out that "hair matching" is often used to link defendants to crime scenes, but there is no uniform standard stating the number of features two strands of hair must share in order to be a match. This means that hair matching, rather than being scientific, is based on experience and opinion. The NAS called for new independent research in many fields of forensic science, along with uniform standards of scientific accuracy for forensic evidence in court cases.

The NAS report is "a major turning point in the history of forensic science in America," says attorney Barry Scheck. He is one of the founders of the Innocence Project, an organization that has helped more than two hundred people get out of prison because DNA tests or other evidence proved that they had not committed the crimes for which they had been convicted.

Harry Edwards, a judge who was one of the leaders of the NAS committee, agrees that changes are needed in the nation's crime labs. "We determine whether people are innocent or whether they are guilty in part based on forensic science evidence, so as a nation it is terribly important to us that we do it as well as it can be done," he says. "And we are not doing it as well as it can be done right now." The fact that forensic science could be improved, however, doesn't mean that no good forensic science is performed in crime laboratories. Peter Marone, head of a group of forensics organizations, was also a member of the NAS committee. In his view, "the great majority of labs are doing first-rate work top to bottom, and make an enormous contribution to public safety."

Forensic science is here to stay. Over the years, forensics has come to play a major role in many crime investigations and court cases, and the crime laboratory is a valuable tool for justice. But like any other tool, the crime lab will be most useful if we fully understand what it can (and cannot) do, and if we use it wisely.

▼ GLOSSARY

autopsy a medical examination performed on a body to find the cause of death; a forensic autopsy also tries to establish the time and manner of death

chain of custody a written record of the history of each piece of evidence from crime scene to trial, with information about everyone who has handled the evidence and why

criminalistics the scientific study of the physical evidence from crime scenes

defendant in a legal case, the person charged with committing a crime or offense

defense in a legal case, the side that represents the person charged with a crime or offense and tries to prove that person is innocent

DNA deoxyribonucleic acid, the substance that contains each individual's genetic code and is found in blood, saliva, and other tissues from the body

DNA testing the use of DNA to identify individuals; DNA testing may also match a person to a piece of evidence or establish a relationship between two individuals

exemplar The known half of a comparison, such as a fingerprint or DNA profile from someone whose identity is known; the exemplar can be compared with a piece of evidence from an unknown source

forensic science the use of scientific knowledge or methods to investigate crimes, identify suspects, and try criminal cases in court

forensics in general, debate or review of any question of fact relating to the law; often used to refer to forensic science

homicide murder

medical examiner (ME) a public official responsible for determining cause of death; the position requires medical training

morgue a special medical facility, usually part of a hospital or forensic lab, where bodies are stored and autopsies are performed

prosecution in a legal case, the side that represents the state; the prosecution charges a person with an offense and tries to prove that person's guilt in court

serology the branch of medical and forensic science that deals with blood

toxicology the branch of medical, environmental, and forensic science that deals with drugs, poisons, and harmful substances

▼ FIND OUT MORE

FURTHER READING

Ferllini, Roxana. *Silent Witness*. Buffalo, NY: Firefly Books, 2002.

Fridell, Ron. *Forensic Science*. Minneapolis, MN: Lerner, 2006.

Friedlander, Mark P., Jr., and Terry M. Phillips. *When Objects Talk: Solving a Crime with Science*. Minneapolis, MN: Lerner, 2001.

Funkhluser, John. *Forensic Science for High School Students*. Dubuque, IA: Kendall Hunt, 2005.

Innes, Brian. *DNA and Body Evidence*. Armonk, NY: Sharpe, 2007.

Joyce, Jaime. *Bullet Proof!: The Evidence That Guns Leave Behind*. Danbury, CT: Children's Press, 2007.

Owen, David. *Police Lab: How Forensic Science Tracks Down and Convicts Criminals*. Buffalo, NY: Firefly, 2002.

Platt, Richard. *Forensics*. Boston: Kingfisher, 2005.

Prokos, Anna. *Guilty by a Hair: Real-Life DNA Matches*. Danbury, CT: Children's Press, 2007.

Townsend, John. *Crime Lab Technician*. New York: Crabtree, 2008.

WEBSITES

www.aafs.org/yfsf/index.htm

The website of the American Academy of Forensic Sciences features the Young Forensic Scientists Forum, with information on careers in forensics. The site also links to other Internet resources.

www.bls.gov/opub/ooq/1999/Fall/art01.pdf
The federal government prepared this downloadable six-page guide to "A Career in the Crime Lab" for young people interested in working in forensic science.

www.crimezzz.net/forensic_history/index.htm
The Crimeline page offers a brief timeline of developments in forensic science from prehistory to the present.

www.fbi.gov/hq/lab/labhome.htm
Visit the FBI Crime Lab at this site, which explains the work of a dozen different forensic specialists. A "News and Stories" link leads to dozens of articles about forensic investigations at the lab, from cracking codes to reconstructing a shooting.

www.forensicmag.com/
Forensic Magazine's web page features case studies and news about developments in forensic science, including articles about crime labs.

www.sciencenewsforkids.org/articles/20041215/ Feature1.asp
Science News for Kids offers "Crime Lab," a brief overview of forensic science, with emphasis on the role of laboratory technicians.

▼ BIBLIOGRAPHY

The author found these books and articles especially helpful when researching this volume.

Cohle, Stephen, and Tobin Buhk. *Cause of Death: Forensic Files of a Medical Examiner*. Amherst, NY: Prometheus Books, 2007.

Houde, John. *Crime Lab: A Guide for Nonscientists*. Ventura, CA: Calico, 2006.

James, Stuart H., and Jon J. Nordby. *Forensic Science: An Introduction to Scientific and Investigative Techniques*. 2nd edition. Boca Raton, FL: Taylor & Francis, 2005.

Kelly, John F., and Philip K. Wearne. *Tainting Evidence: Inside the Scandals at the FBI Crime Lab*. New York: Free Press, 2002.

Moore, Solomon. "Science Found Wanting in Nation's Crime Labs." *New York Times*, February 4, 2009, online at www.nytimes.com/2009/02/05/us/05forensics.html?_r=2

National Research Council of the National Academies. *Strengthening Forensic Science in the United States: A Path Forward*. Washington, DC: National Academies Press, 2009, available online at www.nap.edu/catalog.php?record_id=12589

Neme, Laurel A. *Animal Investigators*. New York: Scribner, 2009.

Teichroeb, Ruth. "Rare look inside state crime labs reveals recurring DNA test problems." *Seattle-Post-Intelligencer*, July 22, 2004, online at www.seattlepi.com/local/183007_crimelab22.html

U.S. Department of Justice. *Forensic Laboratories: Handbook for Facility Planning, Design, Construction, and Moving.* Washington, DC: Department of Justice, Office of Justice Programs, 1998.

Zonderman, Jon. *Beyond the Crime Lab: The New Science of Investigation.* New York: Wiley, 1999.

▼ INDEX

▼ ABOUT THE AUTHOR

REBECCA STEFOFF is the author of many books on scientific subjects for young readers. In addition to writing previous volumes in the Forensic Science Investigated series, she has explored the world of evolutionary biology in Marshall Cavendish's Family Trees series; she also wrote *Robot* and *Camera* for Marshall Cavendish's Great Inventions series. After publishing *Charles Darwin and the Evolution Revolution* (Oxford University Press, 1996), she appeared in the *A&E Biography* program on Darwin and his work. Stefoff lives in Portland, Oregon. You can learn more about her books for young readers at **www.rebeccastefoff.com**.